About this booklet

The aim of the Women's Oral History Group Lesbian Identity Project has been to record and preserve accounts of lesbian life. Because the lives of lesbians have so often been hidden from history, we decided to document the life-stories of some lesbians at the turn of the twentieth century. We began an oral history project and interviewed over thirty women of different ages about their lives and perceptions on the development of their lesbian identity.

The oldest woman interviewed was born in 1926, the youngest in 1970. Their lives have spanned most of the twentieth century and into the twenty-first. They lived through a period of enormous social, economic and technological change. For much of this time lesbians have been 'invisible'; their feelings, opinions and actual existence have been ignored in the mass media.

We felt it was very important for the women to tell their stories in their own way with minimum intrusion from the interviewers. We are very grateful to those women who were willing to share their experiences with us.

The recordings were transcribed and we decided to produce a series of booklets in a thematic presentation of quotations from the interviews. This is the fourth and last in the series. The first booklet was: 'Lesbians … and Christianity', the second: 'Lesbians on … Choosing Our Icons', and the third: 'Lesbians on … Becoming Our Selves'.

A brief account of the Women's Oral History Group Project itself is included at the end of this booklet.

In this booklet we present accounts of the daily lives of lesbians. The first theme covered is homophobia and the interviewees' experiences of bigotry and prejudice. Next we present recollections of gay and lesbian groups, equal rights and other political movements in which the women played a part and which contributed to their lesbian identity. And finally, we record what women said and felt about lesbian life, the communities and networks which they helped set up and to which they belonged.

LIP Lesbian Identity Project   **Women's Oral History Group**

Lesbians on ...

Living Our Lives

Lesbian Identity Project

Published in the United Kingdom by LIP Publishing.

© LIP 2011

ISBN: 978-0-9561331-3-7

Designed by frogsdesign, Hebden Bridge

Printed by H Charlesworth & Co Ltd, Wakefield

LOTTERY FUNDED

Contents

Introduction: About this booklet   3

Section 1: Homophobia   7

    Overt homophobia   9

    Childhood and early memories   9

    Women's experience of homophobia as adults   11

    Lesbian invisibility   17

    Responses to homophobia   18

Section 2: Causes and Campaigning   25

    Gay and lesbian campaigning   27

    The second-wave women's movement   30

    Wider campaigning: from personal to global issues   35

Section 3: Lesbian networks and communities   39

    Finding other lesbians   41

    The scene: clubs and pubs   44

    Lesbian networks: belonging and identity   48

Conclusions   56

Glossary   58

Appendix I: The interviews   60

Appendix II: Our Oral History Project – The Group's process   62

    Notes   64

I got teased remorselessly

... so for two years I was trying to suppress my lesbian feelings

... they were beating us up, for being dykes

... she wasn't going to employ me because I was lesbian

... we had a lot of homophobic hate crime

Homophobia

In this section the women we interviewed relate their experiences of homophobia and its effects on them. When older participants in the Project were growing up, male homosexual acts were illegal. It was not until 1967 that this oppressive law was repealed, by which time those born in the 1920s and 30s would be entering middle-age. Given the climate of opinion, how did lesbians feel?

During the interviewees' lives there were very real consequences of being seen as a lesbian. It was not just about attitudes in the decades from the 1930s to the end of the century. For some women the price of being honest was loss of job, status, children, home and finances. Some women were beaten up because of it.

Also, although a girl or woman may not have been directly involved in a homophobic incident, simply witnessing what had happened could well create feelings of unease, fear and consequent undermining of confidence and self-esteem.

When thinking about homophobia directed at lesbians, it is difficult to disentangle the contempt for women pervasive in a misogynistic society such as Britain, from that aimed at female homosexuals. Despite the law reforms of the 1960s which tried to ensure equal rights in Britain, all women faced a degree of oppression. Historically, it is well to remember that until quite recently most authority figures and people in senior positions in public life were male. In the law, the police, the armed forces, the church, medicine and the mass media and in many types of employment there was systemic sexism.

For lesbians there was an additional stigma. Antagonism would manifest itself in a range of ways, from a sense of disapproval surrounding homosexuality, to what is termed institutionalised homophobia – a prejudice against people who were homosexual which was embedded in many of society's structures. Some women analysed what was happening, others said they accepted the status quo for years.

We are aware from the quotations that this process has been painful and often negative. However, many of the women interviewed showed considerable strength and tenacity in overcoming this and getting through to achieve in many fields.

Overt homophobia

Childhood and early memories

Some women spoke of the messages about lesbians that they were exposed to as children and how these often had a negative connotation, whether overt or subtle. Others encountered bullying by other pupils at school. They describe their feelings of isolation and lack of support and how the school dealt with lesbian issues.

Cas, b. 1949, *remembered two women who were neighbours in her childhood:* I think they must have been my first dykes that I ever knew. But we weren't supposed to go anywhere near them or talk to them at all. … All the kids – weren't allowed near them at all.

Interviewer: *Did anybody say why?*
Cas: No. But it was done – it was done in the same way as you would say, don't talk to a stranger. That kind of way. And then it was really – that was something really awful that you just didn't do. So they were my first – I think, now, looking back.

And then the only other gay thing was around, you know, men that had lisps, that were called 'ponces', you know, or 'poofters'. So, you know, that was the other thing.

Lesley, b. 1958, *recalled bullying at school:*
… I was aged 15 to 16 that last year … and again it was the games teacher I got a crush on – and I got teased remorselessly by this group of friends… and eventually a few times I flared up, … I was just beginning to get into a bit of trouble at school, I was in the top class, I was quite bright but getting into a little bit of trouble just because I was seen to be involved in these sort of scuffles – then there was a big fight …

I got very badly beaten up by this girl who was part of my friendship group – I think partly 'cause I wouldn't stop fighting but she was much bigger than me and much taller than me. I ended up – being knocked unconscious, having a bleeding nose, a split lip and stuff, got taken home, – where my mum was really upset at what'd been happening, couldn't tell her why. … What I remember is being very isolated and very, not knowing where to look and what to do and who to talk to and things, …

What happened as a result of that fight was, we got called into the head-mistress and nobody said why the fight had been going on and I *certainly didn't*. I got separated into a different class from all these women, which I didn't think was very fair, …

Lesley talked about legal discrimination and public notions about lesbians in terms of poor sexology (scientific research into sexual matters) that was not evidence-based and created stereotypes. In the early 1980s she went to a lesbian history night class:

Obviously people saw history repeating itself. Section 28 came out either when the class was going on or we continued meeting for a couple of years, … and all of those issues were around.

… Other things that have really been quite important to me, was finding out that Havelock Ellis, who was a quite – a well-known writer on sexuality, … But his study [of lesbians], which is world-renowned, was based on four women, one of whom was his wife, and none of whom actually fitted some of the assertions he made about lesbians. For example, one of the things he said was lesbians often wore manly clothing and smoked cigars or pipes, lesbians were not very good at sewing and all of these things. It's just amazing that something based on such a small study would get such … a reputation, really.

… I found a card recently in my local doctor's surgery, they had a display by Mind … particularly aimed at young lesbians and gay men, and it was quite positive, … but I had a mixed reaction because it was all under this banner that said 'mental health', which sort of took me back to my child-hood or my adolescence where I was fairly desperate, really, and – was looking for emotional and mental health support.

Megan *b. 1966 lived in Australia. Of her schooldays in late 1970s/early 80s, she said:*

I got a right lot of bullying for being a lesbian. … it was because I wasn't behaving towards them [the boys] the way that they thought I should, and I wasn't interested in them, I mean I was just interested in my studies really. … so their way of – teasing me and bullying me was to call me a lesbian but, I couldn't sort of work out why it was that they did that.

But – over those months that I was there it sort of escalated and escalated, and so – it was difficult for me to have – I did have some girls that I was friends with but they sort of became twitchy about – being too close to me because they didn't want to be identified as being a lesbian as well. So that all got quite messy, really.

... Just after I left there was a big scandal because two – two young women were found out to be having a lesbian relationship, and they were, um, the school really came on top of them like a ton of bricks.

... And what happened was that they were forced to go to school without wearing a school uniform because they'd disgraced the school, ... they were boarders, and their parents lived hundreds of miles away, and – they – had to go around every school day not wearing [uniform]- it was a bit like, – wearing scarlet, a scarlet letter, ... they were the only girls, – that weren't wearing uniform and they had to go and stand in front of assembly, the whole school, and tell the school *why* they weren't allowed to wear the uniform and they were really publicly humiliated.

And so I imagine they would have been scarred for life.

Colette, *b. 1957. Speaking about her early 20s:*
And I remember buying the *Gay Times*, the *Gay News* for 20p and my grandmother found it in my bedroom and said, 'What the hell are you doing reading this muck?' ... And she was quite derogatory about it – [said] 'Oh, you need seeing to'.

Women's experience of homophobia as adults
Here some interviewees recall how lesbianism was not talked about much in public yet that very fact would mean that there was a sense of disapproval surrounding the topic. Others describe the attitudes to and treatment of lesbians in a variety of public institutions: the law, medicine, armed forces and the police, which caused considerable distress.

Nadine, *b. 1927. When discussing her life-long partnership, Nadine was asked if she was aware of anything that gave her reservations about having a relationship with a woman, she said:*
I don't think I was aware of it. I mean, it sounds ridiculous but things weren't talked about very much, really, in those days. At least, if they were I didn't notice. So I don't think I ever would have sort of defined it as 'being fond of women'. I mean, I knew I wasn't attracted to men ... I knew there were people who disapproved of very close friendships between women ...

but I couldn't see anything wrong in how *we* were and how I felt. ... but there must have been some ... ambivalence in me about it, I *suppose*, but my feelings were so strong that I managed not to listen to the other part of it.

Chris, *born 1947, went into the armed services. Whilst stationed abroad she was involved in one of the forces' notorious 'witch-hunts' when gay people were hunted down and thrown out. She was sent to see the force psychiatrist:*
At the end of it I said, 'Do you think I *am?*' – I think I might have used 'homosexual' but I don't know. And he said he didn't think I was, he said he thought I was 20, I was young, I'd been influenced and that it were just something that I was going through and that I'd grow out of it, and I said, 'Well ... what will happen, will I be thrown out?' And he said, 'No, I don't think so. I don't – I'm not going to recommend that.' ... I did try for two years to make myself straight after that ...

So for two years I was trying to suppress my lesbian feelings and trying to make myself straight, and I was going with this guy for about six months until I was made corporal. I was sent to another camp for training and immediately fell for the female sergeant. I realised I couldn't pretend anymore.

It took me ages to get promoted. I'd got all the qualifications to be pro-moted and I was seeing all these other people promoted that hadn't been in as long as me. And that wasn't how it was meant to work. So I went to see the station adjutant and I said, 'Well, why am I not getting promoted?' and they said, 'Because of what happened – you need a two-year clean slate before you'll get any promotion.' ... So that added the pressure for me to pretend I was straight.

... I'd been in six years and I faced this choice, do I come out of the forces or do I stay ...? I got involved in another witch-hunt, and narrowly escaped being found out, being caught.

... Once I'd slept with this woman, I was then in a dilemma, that I realised that I couldn't stay ... It was some level of acceptance that, yes, I was one of them and that therefore I didn't want to carry on leading a double life. I wanted to come out of the forces and see where I could go, plus the longer I stayed in the more likely it was that I was going to get caught anyway and get thrown out ... Oh gosh, it was a big choice, yes! Because I liked it. I actually liked the forces ... The reason I left was because of my lesbianism. Because I knew that I would get caught – sooner or later.

Sylvia, b. 1952, spoke of her experience of the medical profession:
My partner's got a disability and ... – I know we both, ... have been in hospital, and they've been fairly okay, fairly okay about putting each other down as next-of-kin.

The one time when I realised how ... how much they didn't really accept different relationships was when my partner was actually told the diagnosis that she had [long-term debilitating illness]... they asked me to leave the room while they told her. So I wasn't actually in the room when they told her that. And yet I knew that that's what they were going to tell her, because I'd guessed that's what the situation was. And that shocked me, really, because I'm sure had it been a married heterosexual couple they would have not asked me to leave the room, but they would have definitely said, 'You must be in the room', you know, and I think that was – was quite shocking, really.

But on the whole I think... I think apart from that one, I think there have been fairly positive ... sort of, yeah, responses from the medical profession.

Several women mentioned legal difficulties arising out of society's general failure to acknowledge long-term lesbian relationships. Custody of children and adoption were also major concerns.

Doreen, b. 1931:
Back in 1970 ... the biggest difference, like when I wanted a mortgage it was very difficult for a woman to get a mortgage. Now that wasn't fair ... wills ... life insurances and anything you had in one name only, and that was the way to do it in those days.

Veronica, b. 1957:
Several things happened to push me even further back into the closet and this was one of them. A neighbour across the road eloped with another woman, ... He [the husband] went back and got the children ... and he fought his case through the courts and, so I thought, 'Oh my God!'

Referring to the 1990s, Veronica said:
... We've moved on quite a lot now, and even now, – in Social Services, it depends on what agency you're with as to whether they recruit you as an adoptive parent, so some, even now, aren't as liberated. They weren't as liberated [then] as they are now.

Frances, b. 1953. Asked how her lesbian identity had impacted on other aspects of her life, Frances replied:
Well I think it could have impacted quite severely on my life as a mother because there was at the time (1970s, early 80s) a lot around lesbians losing their children and, you know, I was very fearful of that ... I mean it hasn't happened and it didn't - you know it didn't happen. But that does – does have an impact on you if you're a mother.

Some women spoke about their experience of the police and of the treatment they received specifically as lesbians, an indication of what some men thought about lesbians.

Terri, b. 1941. In the 1980s:
Then we organised the lesbians' conference, the first lesbian conference in London and that was an amazing day, really, ... Had a disco in the evening and at the end of the disco the police staged an incident outside which we got involved with, unwittingly, and I bit a policeman and was arrested, and that was a very scary experience for me.

It was like, I was very angry, – and it drew me closer to some of the women, but it was – it was a very traumatic experience, – being physically abused, shoved up against a van with me arms behind me back and threatened, and other women getting their glasses smashed, trodden on, and thrown around and ... [the] NPG I think they used to be called – like plain clothes police. There were two big vanloads of them who just descended on us, they were waiting for us to come out.

And they were violent, they were really violent, and there were several serious injuries, and it was because we were lesbians, and that went to court and it was very traumatic. There were a lot of – very scary experiences, really.

Megan, b. 1966, lived in Australia:
I went to my first queen's ball in Brisbane, which was sort of like the big drag queen's ball [of the year] and everybody gets dressed up and ... it just blew my mind being in this place, just full of – gay men and women all dressed up, except that as you went down the street to go to this venue every single side street had a police squad car in it. ... you knew that it was like police everywhere.

And when X and I – my girlfriend – when we left, we walked down the stairs and there was a car parked at the bottom of the steps, … so there was two blokes in the front and two women in the back. As they saw us come out, the two blokes got out and they were beating us up, for being dykes, – there were policemen standing on the footpath watching us getting beaten up. And I knew that if I – as soon as I turned round and if I took a swing or if I tried to fight back, that they would arrest me straight away for assault, I knew that that's what they were waiting for, but – *we* managed to get away, so it was okay, but, you know, it was just like that.

… there was only one main gay bar in Brisbane, – and you wouldn't come out on your own because numerous women'd get picked up by the police when they'd left. They'd drive them around the back streets of Brisbane and – have a go at them for being a lesbian and say, – 'We can rape you any time, we know where you live', and all that stuff, and end up dump[ing] them out the vehicle again.

Prejudice in employment

Caitlin *b. 1957, made the link between sexism and homophobia:*
I just burnt myself out with trade union politics, which is a very patriarchal – It's been merely another reawakening, I think. No. Men – despite the fact that over seventy per cent of the membership is female it [is] the men who dominate the positions, it is the men who have that power. And believe you me, they undermine you. Especially when they find out about your sexuality.

Megan *moved from Australia to the UK and recounts her experience:*
Oh, years ago now I went for a job down in [the west country], and when I went for the job interview the woman who was interviewing me at one point asked me if I was a lesbian, and so I said 'Yes', but I said, 'I don't see what … what relevance that has.'

And she also asked me whether I was vegetarian, at one point, and I said, 'No'. [She said] 'You have to do meat inspecting as part of the job.' … Anyway, she said at the end of the interview that, – she had no qualms I'd be able to do the job and that I would be good at my job, but she wasn't going to employ me because I was lesbian.

As well as institutionalised homophobia, at an individual level some women suffered physical aggression and verbal abuse from family, neighbours and the community. *The price of acknowledging that they were lesbian was high, the consequences could be severe, as these examples show.*

Veronica, *lived with her partner:*
We had a lot of homophobic hate crime. Had an awful lot – Well, we were never out, we lived our lives quite normally. …just did what everybody else did, but because we were different on the street we had a lot – we had number plates ripped off, we had ... stuff daubed on the windows, we had stuff thrown through the windows, we had a For Sale sign thrown through the window, from up the road, – verbal – [aggression] …And we ended up in Court.

And all that added to the stress and she [her partner] never wanted to have the relationship recognised, really. For me it was as valid as any other, I never felt ashamed of it and I wasn't bothered that people knew, even though for all those years I suppose I'd got to a stage where I couldn't give a damn, 'cause I'd suppressed everything that I felt.

Cas, *b. 1949, married and had a child. In her mid-thirties Cas acknowledged openly that she was a lesbian:*
Then – then I came home and sat Y (husband) down and told him, and he went berserk. Beat the shit out of me. Cracked my jaw – er, cheekbone. Just this understanding guy I'd spent thirteen years with, so he became, – a kind of maniac, really. So there was no turning back after that.

Cas describes the difficulties:
I never had any money – even though I worked, it went into a joint account, so I never had a sense of having my own money.

… Well, it was a big thing, you know, I was quite ill, it made me ill, before I – left. 'Cause I left this suburb – this beautiful three-storey house, and this nice communal life, – everybody knew where I lived and that. Couldn't do guides and brownies any more 'cause Y (husband) said he was going to tell them.

And I couldn't do community work 'cause Y was going to tell everyone I was a lesbian and their daughters were – at risk. So – I couldn't do my job, because they knew I'd been there, they knew Y, … and he was being quite abusive with phone calls and turning up at the office, and it just became impossible for me to work. So it meant leaving a job that was – that had supported me all those years as well. So I had to do all that, …

16

It was weird, it was like suddenly everything seemed to have taken a long time to change but then all of a sudden it had changed. And I didn't know what my identity was. I had no role any more. I wasn't a worker, I wasn't a mother and I wasn't a wife. And it was all right saying 'lesbian' but what did it mean, you know?

Lesbian invisibility

Women also spoke of much more subtle messages about lesbianism. These took the form of omissions, denial, silences and stereotyping, and the effect this had on them. The Lesbian Identity Project (this oral history project) came into being because of the 'invisibility' of lesbian women in history.

Some participants spoke about general attitudes they encountered. Others spoke of the lack of understanding and stereotyping of lesbians they had experienced both in their private lives and in the mass media generally.

Discrimination made it much harder for women to find ways of meeting other lesbians, in contrast with what was taken for granted for heterosexuals. They revealed their anxiety and ambivalence about being open.

Doreen, b. 1931:
It's only by word of mouth that people can ... get to know other people, in a way, ... You can walk into places and feel like for like and you can get talking and you will *know* ... deep down, but there again, sometimes they're too scared to say anything, and you won't say anything either! So, you know, it's sort of Catch 22.

Noreen, b. 1937, describes trying to contact other women in the 1960s:
'The Evening Post' ... I once tried to put – place an advert in that, and a discreet advert I might add, and they would not accept it.

And then later the frustrating thing is, I was willing – well, I did of course pay for it, I put one in, but they wouldn't specify that I just wanted a *woman* friend, they put 'A woman seeking a friend' and they would not specify – they were afraid of their reputation at the time, they would not specify that I was looking for a woman friend. Well, the result of that was farcical because I got a load of letters from prisoners.

Responses to homophobia

Many women spoke of the presumption of heterosexuality and pressure to present a public image as heterosexual; they reflected on how this has affected them psychologically and socially. Derogatory comments had influenced women's decisions about 'coming out' and being open about their feelings and relationships especially at work or where children were involved.

Doreen *b. 1931, describes one of the earliest efforts at educating the public in the mass media:*

So in '67, ... [the] BBC wanted to do a programme, and I was on that programme and it was done at the Gates [Gateways Club in London]. ...We were sitting around a table and I was smoking like a chimney – nerves, I don't smoke! ... But we were trying to get across – because at that particular time the media were taking the mickey ... out of it [i.e. homosexuality]. At least, this is what I felt.

So we were sitting there trying to explain the situation the way we saw it, and putting it in inverted commas, "normal". We said, 'We're people first. We're human beings. When we go through our front door and close that door – that's it, it's got nothing to do with *anybody else.*'

But the biggest thoughts then [in the 1960s] were that we were corrupting people, ... Now, the biggest laugh is – I would have said – sixty, sixty-five, seventy per cent of teachers, nurses, police force, army were gay - Now, – I can't speak for men – on the women's side, women on the whole are not into young children at all. And presumably, I would say, that is the mothering instinct in us. Therefore there was no sign of corruption, women weren't there to do that. At least, this was how *we* felt. This was what we were trying to get over on that programme. Whether we did or not, I do not know.

In the 1990s, **Veronica** *led a workshop as part of her work:*

[It was] on Sexuality, Gender and Identity and [I] stood in front of a room full of people explaining. ... I allowed them to question me, on my sexuality, ... they'd asked me things like, 'When you walk into a room full of women, do you go "Cor!"'

... I [had] said to this woman, 'Well, do you do it with men?' 'Yeah.' 'Well, then, why should I be any different?' 'Yes, I do like women and I do look at women and think, "Cor, she's nice," you know. But it doesn't mean I want to go to bed with her.'

And, 'Do you fancy all women?' 'Well, no. Do you fancy all men?' 'Do you fancy married women?' And I said, 'Well, sometimes, but do you fancy married men?' 'Well, sometimes.' I said, 'Well, I have morals and standards just like everyone else and it much depends on what you do about that at the end of the day, whether you're heterosexual or whether you're gay or lesbian.'

It's like a thought process and they don't think it through, they just – just have this idea that you're a very sexual being, that you'll pursue everything that walks past you! And they were saying, 'Oh, we never thought that through.'

Chris born 1947, remembered a landmark of 1968:
The Killing of Sister George came out, and I went to the pictures to see the film with this girl that I fancied. Oh, my God! I'm sittin' there and sweat's pouring off me!

… When I saw that film – it *frightened* me… And I tell you, it wasn't the main character frightened me, the person who frightened me was the woman who played the boss, … And she went in to chat up … the younger one … That scared me stiff because she was predatory. …Didn't stop me being lesbian but it frightened me, I remember. A lot of it I found exciting, but I remember that scene really frightened me.

Una, b. 1940:
I think I've always been on the fringe, I've never really joined, because it's – I couldn't, I couldn't – I couldn't play the game, you know. I have played the game actually, very steadily all the way through but I couldn't play it that amount by joining in the heterosexual groups.

… I tell you, I've just joined a [leisure] group here and, very nice people, … but it's amazing as we sit there, the sexual innuendoes that go on and tittering around the room, … – and I just sit there and, … I'm on the outside of it, … And I get sick of – it's amazing how much sexual talk goes around. I mean, in the [another group] I'm in, again, there's all sorts of sexual innuendoes in the talk, very indirect some of it. And it – what one has to do is kind of vaguely join in or smile vaguely, – at the jokes … and sort of, just to fit, that you're, – part of this thing.

19

But it got – it really got me down when I was – [in the] 1980s … and in the end I decided I couldn't stand it any longer, … and the whole cultural thing, the heterosexual thing, sort of did me in and I thought, – I can't cope with this any longer, really. And changed careers at that point, into a career where it was much better.

Rosemary, b. 1934, reflected on 'coming out':
It's such a restricting life, though, not to come out. I would advise *anybody* to do it now. Because you are living a *lie*. And it means you have to slightly change your vocabulary … to avoid … you talk about 'my friend who I usually go on holiday with' or something like that! … I very rarely refer to her as my partner, even now.

At work: I got to fairly senior positions, but whether I would have got there had I been openly gay – or whether, looking at it the other way, I would have been more successful because I didn't have to tell lies and would actually have done even better, is quite an interesting thought.

Georgina, b. 1951, considers the impact of homophobia and her feelings about being open about sexual orientation:
But, – I approached things a bit cautiously. You know, specially if I'm a bit frightened and I *was* frightened of coming out as a lesbian, about what other people's reactions would be.

…I did – though, get myself into a couple of situations at work, or was put into, I don't know that I got myself into them, that were – discriminatory, really.

… But I have to say as well that each time I come out explicitly as a lesbian in a public sector, in a public setting, part of me has this fear or anxiety inside me. Each time there's part of me that feels - my heart starts beating 'n' I think, 'God', which – is to do with the anxiety and fear, and conversely I always feel it's a very strong thing to do and a sort of joyful thing to do as well.

So I get both those feelings … the joy is clearly there very deep but so is the fear really. And I don't expect that to change 'cause it's still there even though I feel, quite confident in my work life, in my private life, in my family life … my community life, but, I mean, one of the things places where I haven't done it is [as] a school governor of our local primary school, …

I have not made it explicit and I will be very careful about that because I do not wanna expose myself to my imagined fantasies of what some ... parents and teachers might feel towards lesbians, and I know that's – a fantasy, but, ... I would hope it does happen but I will be very careful about how it happens that I come out there ... if at all. ... That's the whole thing about children and lesbianism and adults, heteros – you know, the hetero-sexual adult fears ... misinformation, prejudice and all that stuff.

Some women spoke of the difficulty in accepting their own feeling for another woman because of how this was seen at the time. This led many to speak in emotional terms about a deep internal conflict. This has sometimes been referred to as 'internalised homophobia'. Interviewees also made the point that internal-ised homophobia ran deep and it was difficult to overcome.

Several reported they felt pressure to conceal their relationships with other women. And some, when they became aware of prejudice and homophobia, were pushed back into 'the closet' – into hiding their real life and relationships.

Olive, *b.1934, on living with a partner in the 1960s:*
I was very *aware* of other people living in the kind of relationship that obviously I was living in, and I think we probably spent an awful lot of time and energy concealing [it] -rather than exposing.

Veronica, *b. 1957, spoke about her gradual realisation:*
I think I got hold of some literature from somewhere, I don't know where that came from, whether I got it in a bookshop or something, and I was thinking, well, people don't obviously agree with this.

You know, it kind of dawned on me about homophobia and all that sort of stuff after that, that all sort of fell into place over the next few years and – it kind of dawned on me that, – God Almighty .... That's the last thing you do. Tell anybody. So that kind of pushed me right in the closet and I decided I'd just made my bed and I have – I would have to lie on it.

Zoe, *b. 1964, spoke about the development of her public identity as a lesbian and her experiences of living in the provinces and large cities:*
And I think [there] was a stage in my life that I needed, to mix with like-minded people. For me, that was quite a big important thing, that I could walk down the street holding hands with the person that I'm in love with. Whereas now I would sort of link arms. Like girls do. And it's not looked at...

What's interesting since I've come to Z (large Midlands city) I've gone nowhere near the gay scene here in Z. I don't feel the need to. I am intrigued as to what it's all about, but going into the city centre women hold hands. It's a place where people are okay. You are what you are, and they're not suddenly going to start pointing at you or shouting names at you.

Sylvia b. 1952, spoke about falling in love in her early 20s:
I had a struggle … bearing in mind I was doing Religious Education. So there was this huge struggle … not sort of understanding where this was coming from, thinking that we were the only two in the whole wide world. … In my head … was what we were feeling, doing, you know, was wrong. I mean, the word 'lesbian' was something I couldn't say, I couldn't look at myself in the mirror.

In the 1980s I really looked at the political elements around it [lesbianism], that's when I became really strong within myself.

Chris, b. 1947, on her lesbian identity:
You know having been involved with lesbian politics for sixteen-plus years, I don't think that's helped with my internalised homophobia. There's still some there, I've got to be honest and say there is, and I don't know whether I will ever get rid of – totally get rid of it. Because there's times when I just don't – you know, I don't … I don't want to be seen in public holding my partner's hand.

Ruby, b.1970, commented on how a lack of awareness and education about sexuality can place an additional burden on lesbian or gay people in wider groups:
At college – I had no problems being out but I had a lot of homophobia within the course, and (I was training to be a Community Worker) and there was very low awareness, [about] sexuality. There were other lesbian and gay people on the course but I got to be sort of [known] and – everything I did became about sexuality, …

… I've known a lot of lesbians … who were doing the same course – I know that they've all done that, every year. You know, every year there's been a fight about it and every year lesbians have … educated their peer group, like I did.

… So unless there's lesbians – students there, (or gay men but mostly it tends to be lesbians), pushing it, then it doesn't become part of the curriculum. And the reason why I'm so mad about it is because it's community development workers, it's not accountants, you know! Accountants! it'd probably be useful to be able to go to a lesbian accountant but it's not like a life or death sort of thing like it is with community work where – you're training people to deal with oppression and they don't get around [to] sexuality, and so – my colleagues and my profession are not particularly sort of up [front] – about it. And that, - that maddens me.

In terms of the roots of both external and internalised homophobia, a lot of women spoke of their often (but not always) negative experiences of Christian churches. 'Lesbians… and Christianity' is the subject of the first in our series of booklets…

Judith, *b. 1934, recalls speaking to a Church of England official, (the head of X Diocese Board for Social Responsibility), in 1970s:*
And then I took a deep breath and I did the maddest thing in my life; I said, 'Well, there is something else that the Church could do and that is to look into its views on homosexuality, and I am a homosexual and I find it extremely difficult … hearing the Church doesn't support and is obviously down on me as a person … I hate it.' So he brought me into training sessions with the clergy.

Judith's experience demonstrates the value and a positive result of speaking out. In this Section we have presented quotations which recount the individual and social cost of homophobia. In the next Section we present accounts of how individuals challenged the status quo, of how they took affirmative action.

I came to feminism through lesbianism

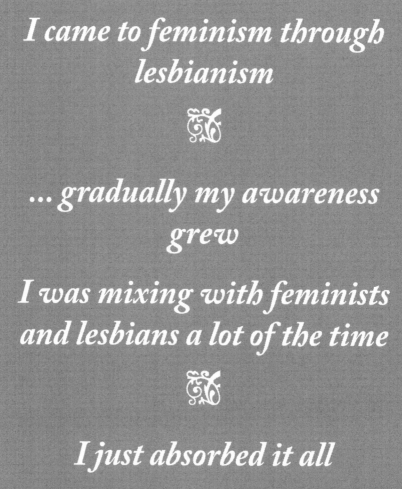

... gradually my awareness grew

I was mixing with feminists and lesbians a lot of the time

I just absorbed it all

I began to meet other lesbians ... huge relief!

Causes and campaigning

In our second section participants recall the various political movements, organisations, groups and campaigns in which they were, and still are, involved.

Illustrating the development of lesbian identity has been a key aim of our Project. Some aspects of identity are given and not amenable to change, for example, age and ethnicity. Others, such as type of education or geographical location, have an impact on an individual growing up, but might be outside her control. However, where there is choice an individual's decisions will be important.

While some may remain detached from political engagement for many reasons, others will take action. How does an individual set about translating her feelings of powerlessness, injustice or inequality into positive action? How does she go about working for equality and a fairer society?

It may seem to be stating the obvious but history is significant here. For example, the twentieth century saw the ebb and flow, progress and retrenchment in the long struggle for women's rights. The equal rights campaigns of the 1960s onwards created many possibilities for involvement and action. Such chances would not have been so apparent in previous decades. Several of the extracts reflect that situation.

The participants show the methods they adopted. Some extracts track a clearly-defined politicisation process, others less so. The ways and means of women's informal networking are revealed.

Many women were active in several gay and lesbian organisations. Activism in second-wave feminism was significant, particularly for those who became adults during the mid-1960s to 1990s, while others took part in peace campaigning. In so doing, these women were part of the history of the fight against oppression in Britain throughout the twentieth century.

Gay and lesbian campaigning

Many women became founders or members of groups and organisations campaigning for gay and equal rights or groups active in the gay community. They ran training courses educating the public on sexuality and gender, homophobic awareness and equal rights; others worked in trades unions and public authorities to promote equality. Some ran Lesbian Lines, or other contact organisations such as NOLN. They organised or attended lesbian conferences, history groups and classes. Many went on Gay Pride marches, demonstrations opposing Clause 28, or belonged to groups such as the Gay Liberation Front and Lesbian and Gay Christian Movement.

Rosemary, b. 1931, describes her activities:
I got involved in Women in Media, which was a group which ran for a time in London, and I did there run into Jackie Forster, who was of course well known and lovely and awfully nice – a gay woman. … It was the seventies by the time I got involved. We had a thing called Women's Action Day, which must have been in about [early 1970s].

I was living in London and, and … I met X. Now it was X who brought me in to – much more, to gay circles. … We did go on a march together, wearing pink badges – and of course – that certainly would have brought it all out into the open – would have made my sexuality known …

Sally, b. 1951, came out in the mid-1980s:
I'm always sad that I was such a wimp because I'd missed the kind of radicalism of the seventies, but that would fit with me because I see myself as a lesbian first and a feminist [second]. I didn't come to lesbianism through feminism, I came to feminism through lesbianism. I think there's quite a strong difference there. It was always within, it wasn't outside influences really.

I gave up work and went to college … and I'm working in – research which is around violence against women and children … so coming out as a lesbian was the – politicising of me.

Sylvia b. 1952, reflected:
It's really funny, a lot of lesbians I've met say that – they were feminists first – actually – and then became lesbians. I was *definitely* a lesbian first

and then became a feminist. I mean, to me they go hand in hand. Some-one said, feminism is the – the theory of it and lesbianism is the practice! ... And then I threw myself into various causes. I became involved with, driving an ambulance for people with disabilities. So I did things like that, and then I became very involved with the Lesbian Line and I did some – direct action around Clause 28, Section 28.

Although I was a teacher, I recall daubing 'Lesbians Are Everywhere' – around – north Wales! We went out in the middle of the night and – [wrote] 'Stop the Clause' and so on. ... and I guess that was because there was a lot of political activity going on at that time amongst lesbians but, – gay men as well, particularly around Clause 28. ...

Looking back on the early 80s, there were – I can't believe it now, but there were lesbian pubs – lesbian and gay pubs, lesbian and gay clubs [in] north Wales. When I think about one particular – seaside town, late 70s, early 80s, there were certainly three either definitely lesbian and gay pubs or lesbian and gay-friendly pubs.

And I *think* that Section 28 and the sort of repression that came, – with the Tory government certainly had an effect that, – people almost went underground. So there was more like a sub-culture of – of support, and people meeting in each other's houses.

Lesley, b. 1958, described her lesbian history evening class in London in the early 1980s:
That was excellent in what subjects it raised. ... pretty progressive, ... and through that [I] met lots and lots of other lesbians who are still friends today. ... As far as I know it was the first one that was put on in the whole country. And the first year it was taught by two women as tutors ... So they were actually professional historians, and – were interested in both feminist history and lesbian history and the history of sexuality.

... We also kept a class diary, and we did various additional research our-selves to bring to class, ... for example, we were going to look particularly at lesbians in the suffragette movement, and various women would go off to the Fawcett Library [now The Women's Library] and look up and find things, ... magazines from 1910 or whatever, which had all these lesbian issues and articles – which, of course [was] completely mind-blowing, ... Not only were lesbians around, which obviously there would have been, but they had networks and newsletters and social events and things like that, …

The other thing I got involved with in London was the campaign against Section 28, initially Clause 28. … Also because of being in London going to a lot of the Pride events as well, – and therefore issues about the relationship between lesbians and gay men obviously came up. I also did quite a lot of work for the Terrence Higgins Trust, … and that brought me into contact with a lot of gay men as well … previously to that [I] hadn't really had very much contact with … with gay men – and found that clearly we had things in common but also that we were very, very different as well.

Reflecting on the activity in London in the 1980s, Lesley said:

But things were organised from a feminist, lesbian feminist perspective and I don't really see that around any more, – I can remember going to big, big debates about lesbian S and M in London and whether that was an issue that we should be organising against or whether we needed to liberate ourselves! in order to, – free our sexuality. All those kind of debates, and *class* was a big issue then as well, which again I don't hear that same debate in that up-front way any more ...

Chris, b. 1947:
I went on my first Lesbian and Gay Pride march in '79, I think it was – '79, in London. I remember seeing the *GLF* (Gay Liberation Front) on television. So I'd come out, I'd been with my first partner, I was identifying as gay, … and then there was lots of demonstrations on television. They'd come on – in dresses, you know, the men being really camp and wearing make-up and dresses … And I remember feeling embarrassed about it, thinking that they shouldn't be doing that … That – they were making fools of themselves, they were showing themselves off and I didn't feel – I didn't want … to be associated with them at that time … I didn't have anything to do with gay politics then, it was years, years later that I got involved with them.

Isobel, b. 1959. In the late 1980s:
So I went along to – there was *LGCM*, the Lesbian and Gay Christian Movement, run a women's arm called 'Ruth's Night Out' in London, and I went along to that.

Zoe, b.1964, was asked if she had taken part in political action:
No. Mainly because up till ten years ago I was very timid, very shy, wouldn't do that kind of thing, wouldn't have the courage to go into anywhere that I wasn't known.

So I've come up through the gay scene, that has been my stepping stone. … and its not what I'm into now. But for a lot of gay young people now – its what they need. But they'll move away from that. And I think it was a stage in my life that I needed, to mix with like-minded people.

The second-wave women's movement

For quite a few women, feminist beliefs led to participation in some of the great range of activities and campaigning of the 'second-wave' women's liberation movement (approximately late 1960s – 1990).

Alison, b. 1946, describes her feelings in her early twenties:
I was aware that [a] woman somehow got a raw deal and that too much was expected of women and men seemed to get away with a lot. … So anyway I went along to this women's liberation meeting and – people were talking about how they felt oppressed and why and I was scratching my brains to think why. Although I mean it was obvious- really! But – I was so well socialised I didn't *know* why. … I felt that – the men in my life at that time hadn't treated me well, hadn't supported me.

Gradually my awareness grew about the position of women in society and basically how we were oppressed, couldn't express ourselves the same and I started to challenge men about it – I would challenge them about their use of language – like calling women 'birds' and things like that. And I found that the men were very very defensive – 'cos this was fairly early days.

Alison began to travel:
I was getting interested in women's liberation. Friends at work gave me various books to take away with me, so on the Trans-Siberian train I was reading Betty Friedan and Shulamith Firestone! … So I came back from my travels a feminist! …

In the 1970s/early 80s she went to live in a northern provincial city:

The lesbian community was just emerging, really. It was very much tied up with GLF, Gay Liberation Front, which was totally dominated by men, at the time. There was very very few lesbians involved, but I – became one of them! … It was a thriving thing at the time, *GLF*, … So from there I think a lot of stuff for lesbians developed in Y [city], and we started having our own disco separate to the men, women-only discos, and lesbian meetings in pubs and a lot of things really took off.

But I went to women's liberation meetings as well, so I was sort of mixing with feminists and lesbians a lot of the time, consciousness-raising groups and groups wanting to set up.

… I suppose because I very much wanted women to stand on their own two feet and even with gay men I recognised that women would take a back seat …

And then there was a lot going on in Y, particularly in women's liberation area when I moved up, there was a lot of very radical women around, stuff to do with women's health and reproductive rights and then the sort of personal political stuff and a lot of women were coming out as lesbians.

And then there was the big, – sort of radical revolutionary women's movement, which I was only on the fringes of, really. But that gathered a lot of strength, to do with violence against women, and centred around trying to set up a rape crisis centre, and marches in the street against violence against women – which of course grew in number during the Peter Sutcliffe era (*when the serial killer known as the Yorkshire Ripper went undetected in the 1980s*).

Chris *b. 1947. Although she had some involvement with feminist groups, Chris says that she was not influenced by modern feminism:*
Feminism was never my politics. *Never.* Because it never related to my experience either as a lesbian or as working class … but I did identify with the suffragists, who were actually going into factories and talking to working class women … it was the first wave, and it was the radical suffragists rather than the suffragettes … I read a book called DLD, Dykes Loving Dykes, and it was very important that book, because for the first time it identified about working class butch lesbians. There was parts of it that I disagreed very much with, but a lot of it I identified with, so for the first time I'd come across a politics that were meaningful to me.

Mary, b. 1947:
I seem to have missed the women's movement and everything!

Margot, b. 1947. In the early 1970s:
I began to realise that there were women's groups and that women grouped themselves together, and that these consciousness-raising groups etc. and women's liberation actually kind of were like honeypots that lesbians could buzz around. But every time I looked down these listings there was never anything in X [northern city] at all. I thought, 'I'm gonna have to move'.

Caitlin, b. 1957, went to university as a mature student in the late 1970s/ early 80s. She tells how enriching she found it:
And there was radical women's politics, and from the women's university group they were organising women's centres – late 70s, – there was a – Women's Aid had been established in X [northern city] years previous to that. Ohh, it was just amazing, I just walked into all that and it was like osmosis, I just absorbed it all ... just absorbed it all. Very, very much [enriching].

And then going into the 80s, and there were still student grants then. We hadn't an idea what students would have to pay come the mid-90s, because Thatcher had just got into power and there was still in the early 80s a lot of hope, a lot of ideas going on, before her reign really started to grind into us. Before that backlash against women. You know, before all the things that we'd striven for were being clawed away.

Slowly and grindingly she [Thatcher] knocked the hell out of us during the 80s – during the 90s. That's right – '79 till 1990, oh! she ground us down. But meanwhile we thought she couldn't touch us, within the university groups we were still together, still organising, still reading, still – organising around feminist theory, how we live, etcetera.

Frances, b. 1953:
I would define myself as a lesbian feminist. But you must remember this was the sixties and there were lots of other things going on at the same time. Well the alternative culture was coming in, – I considered myself a bit of a rebel in that respect so I was reading all the alternative papers when I could get hold of them ... I think I was led into the sort of whole counter-culture, hippie, – alternative scene.

I joined a women's liberation group. I saw this advert for a women's group in my area, just starting, it was called 'Consciousness Raising'. ... and so I used to go to this group once a week, met with various other women, and we talked about real things! and that was just such a revelation, it was just incredible ...

[This gave me] a political context as well, that was really important, – it did seem like at that point (in 1975) that feminism was the theory and lesbianism the practice and – that made sense. ... I mean at that point we were nearly all lesbians ... so we just got involved in any activity that was going on, there was something called the Women's Monthly Events in London that we used to go to those, met loads of new friends, did loads of actions, ... we did all the abortion rallies and all that – arrested in the Houses of Parliament and all sorts.

But then realising that actually, ... us as lesbians were doing a lot of campaigning around women's issues but not actually very much for ourselves, – and that was kind of a change really.

[At the] same time ... as I was a social worker I was becoming more and more aware of what men do to women ... and that kind of put a different angle on things... so men – [were] starting to become the enemy. ... So different political actions came out of that, ... and the whole notion of political lesbianism came – in at that point – late – seventies ... The friends that I made ... also had children – we all knew each other terribly well and we all supported each other in terms of child care as far as we could and we went on holiday together and all that kind of thing.

And then there was a lot around the difference between feminists and lesbians at some – point. And there was the lesbian culture that involved a lot of bars; and there was the lesbian culture that involved lesbian mothers; Greenham and that kind of action. There were different things – and you became aware [of] that. On the whole, women I was hanging out with probably wouldn't have identified as butch and femme, for example, and there was a different culture where women did do that. ... You became aware; then there was all sorts of arguments around sexuality and forms of sexuality ... that was in the eighties I suppose mainly ...

Natasha, b. 1965, reflected on the need for a 'specific (i.e. feminist) profile' in her work:

I think my sort of socialist feminism would come through in that I do think you need some social identity. Therefore, for instance, I've just written – a training pack for – about lesbian health needs within the local area. That is purely because of my political consciousness and awareness that you actually need to, at certain times, *identify* ... – When push comes to shove, – unless there is – some label attached to something, you're never going to have any social or political movement that's going to be able to get – equal rights, equal opportunities, whatever it is that you're fighting for, for a certain particular group, whether that's lesbians, whether it's black – issues around race, whatever it is.

I think in many ways the gay agenda has over-ridden the lesbian agenda and in some ways I think they're both fighting for the same cause, but I think the gay agenda to me ... is academics playing it up, writing books, making money and making a name for themselves, and whether that's me being hugely cynical I don't know. And also I think once you get into the gay agenda, ... often – you would exclude radical lesbians because they wouldn't want to include men...

Natasha describes studying and research at university:

And reading more about the history of women ... I really started reading a lot more around ... So I think through reading – and then I did my degree – ... a lot of feminist research and it was a feminist perspective that I took. ... That was really when I started to get into feminism; so I was about ... 24, 25 at that stage. And I think through that I suddenly hit this like real radical ... – radical *feminism*, and really wanting to fight for women's rights ... So what I did, I wrote – my thesis ... but it was from a feminist perspective, so it was looking around patriarchy ... That really got me into being more aware of feminist literature but also feminist research, feminist methodology.

Wider campaigning: from personal to global issues

Elizabeth, b. 1926:
I became involved, in about '59, with *CND* (Campaign for Nuclear Disarmament), ... and then I became involved with the direct action wing of the anti-bomb movement. ... some of their people came to contact *CND* groups in the area to try and get support for the demonstrations, and came to see me, ... what flowed from this was that they wanted someone to work in London in the office and asked me if I would.

... I mean, this really was my political awakening, I think, because then I met a lot of different people of all kinds, that I hadn't encountered before. I had to think through not just my attitudes to the nuclear bomb but to war in general, and, as I say, society in general, politics in general. So I started to find out what I really believed, and what was really me.

Una, b. 1940, a describes the various organisations in which she became involved. In the mid-1970s:
I came across the feminist movement in the mid-70s. ... just at that stage *LGCM* (Lesbian and Gay Christian Movement) was getting going, I think, and their magazine came across my desk as part of educating the staff.

... Also very soon after that the Movement for the Ordination of Women Got going. Now – that was huge! I'd be 35 then. At that stage onwards I became much more educated about lots of things really.

... So there was *LGCM* and then there was the women's movement, and there was another group that I joined which was very, very important which was called, Women in Theology ... and we used to have all sorts of weekends and run educational-type things, feminist-type things, which I was very much part of. And it was there that I began to meet other – and in *LGCM*, yes both, I began to meet other lesbians. ... Huge relief!

Some time later:
...we had a group we went camping with, who in a way, weren't – quite on our wavelength, weren't quite as educated as we were really, but it was so nice to have – anybody – really.

... I did once go to Greenham ... for a day. ... a particularly large gathering.

We gradually left LGCM because it was so male, and also High Church and anti-women, ... We went up for the Clause 28 and marched in London for that ... The only march I've ever been on that's to do with lesbian and gay [politics].

Cas, b. 1949, explained that in the 1970s/8s she had been politically active and interested in several movements, for example, in trade unions, campaigns for peace, the Nuclear-Free and Independent Pacific:
So I had a kind of vague interest in feminism ... I'd read a bit about it, didn't understand quite a lot of it, so I missed out on the consciousness-raising, looking at ... your vagina kind of bit, I missed out on that. Otherwise I might have been a dyke earlier!

Because I'd done a lot of work round the anti-Vietnam war, I was interested in Greenham, and Greenham was very much about an anti-militarism stance. Then there was this *feminism* kind of word as well ... I knew the camp had been set up, because there was lots of publicity about it. ... And that first time I went it was mixed (gender) – at Yellow Gate.

... About seven or eight months later ... by then the men had been asked to leave, it was *very* different. I just remember that contrast, between the second time it being so informal, and [we] just sat around the fire for hours and just talked about everything. And I hadn't had conversations like that since I don't know when. Where you could just talk about everything. So in point of fact you weren't talking about your kids, you weren't talking about your husband – some of them were, but there was loads of other things being talked about as well, and I just loved it.

And then there was that realisation that maybe I loved it because – there was no blokes there, – and I wasn't aware then whether there were any lesbians around, because I wasn't actually looking for any lesbians, I was just aware that it was all women.

I've always been non-scene

I thought, 'Right, I'm gonna go for it now'

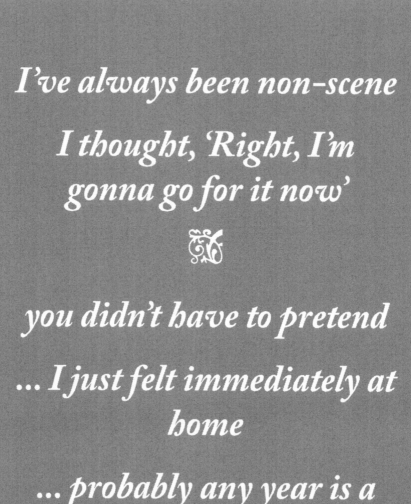

you didn't have to pretend

... I just felt immediately at home

... probably any year is a good time when you come out as a lesbian

Lesbian networks and communities

This section of the booklet covers the social and cultural lives of our interviewees.

The question of how and where participants met other similar women was discussed in most of the interviews. In work and social life generally, there have always been women who were attracted to like-minded women, women who had a similar approach to life and possibly similar sexual feelings; some respondents had experienced this.

These accounts show how in the past women made contacts with other lesbians in a number of ways. Friends, work colleagues, acquaintances working in organisations and campaigns provided 'word-of-mouth' information. In particular, the rise of equal rights campaigning, from the later 1960s on provided opportunities for networking.

What about 'the scene'? The custom of lesbian socialising, often in pubs and clubs, where 'being out' and mixing with many other lesbians provided places to meet and the chance to find lovers and friends. Here there are some vivid descriptions of the historic lesbian scene which flourished under the radar of public awareness. More recently the notion of a lesbian community or communities has become accepted, although looking at main-stream media stories about gay life one still finds little that reflects lesbian life. However there are many groups covering a range of interests from walking to bird watching, and places where women can meet. One of the difficulties lesbians still face is finding out about events and networks. Some areas have newsletters and magazines which reflect life in local communities.

In our previous booklets some comments about lesbian identity show ambivalence. Women said they did not want to be identified solely as lesbian and felt that a 'lesbian' identity was not necessary or particularly appropriate. Yet at the same time they recognised that without some kind of public profile or lesbian visibility, girls and women who are in the early stages of awareness can feel isolated and alone.

Lesbian networks and communities, like all communities, are organic. They grow, change and fade, their social structure alters. Perhaps it is more pertinent to speak about a sense of belonging which leads to varied communities and certainly some of the interviewees speak of "finding" a place to belong.

Finding other lesbians

Noreen, b 1937, describes trying to find like-minded women. She went to a gay pub:
I felt totally out of place – I suppose I envied the ones that were together, the couples – and yet it wasn't my scene, literally it wasn't my scene. And I've always been non-scene.

Olive, b. 1934, said she first became aware of gay politics as part of the political ferment of the 1970s when a colleague mentioned a men's organisation:
It wasn't Gay Pride, … Anyway it was one of the gay organisations that were going on at the time. And he was quite open about these activities and so on. So I thought, 'Good for you!' Although, – I wasn't actually aware of – a lesbian counterpart.

Georgina, b. 1951:
I started going to lesbian things, women-only things and lesbian-only things in London that I heard about. I mean, other people, lesbians I worked with told me about or I heard about them, the discos … for instance, … I'm trying to remember when I went to me first – when I went to a lesbian conference. I used to go from that time on; we had annual women community workers conferences in different parts of the country, and always there would be a lesbians – workshops, that I went to, so that was linked to work, – but was very definitely influenced by – lesbian culture and stuff like that, the sorts of music and – things like that.

Veronica, b.1957 spoke about life in a provincial northern town in the 1990s:
And there wasn't much going on at a local level, at all. 'Cause I was in touch with the Switchboard I knew what was going on, and after about a year one of them told me about *NOLN.*

I started to come to *NOLN.* And since then I've never looked back. In fact, the last three years, you know, I made a network of friends at this end, really. … So I feel like I'm just at the beginning.

Both Lesley and Isobel discussed moving north in the 1990s:

Lesley, b. 1958,:
I then went to X [northern city] for a year and met a lot of lesbians in X, mostly initially through contacts that I'd had from many years ago when

I was involved with Women's Aid and then through that a network of women who knew other women.

I found it very positive for lesbians but also quite difficult to get into. It was a good year to be there because they were fundraising for a women's cultural club, so there were quite a lot of events organised during that time, which were fundraising events but were also fun and enjoyable events. ... And they were mostly organised by lesbians, ...

Isobel, b. 1959:
I didn't sort of go to any of the – any of the lesbian night stuff. You know, the scene stuff, when I was in London. Well, partly ... I didn't have much money.

In 1995 she came north:
That's when I thought, 'Right, I'm gonna go for it now.' I went along to the, – the Lesbian Line thing, and they run – they used to run like an informal social gathering for people who were fairly new – at the Red Lion, and I went along to that a few times, but they were a little bit on the cliquey side, it was hard to break into it, so I didn't stay there for very long.

Laura, b 1961:
So we did have one set of friends who I met through one of my jobs, and spotted, ... as you do! Accurately. No problem. There was – well, – the password there was, 'Do you like kd lang?' 'Oh, yes, I've been meaning to talk to *you!*' Yes, 'cause that was kd lang's main sort of period of promi-nence in this country, and it obviously was the usual password at the time! So that worked.

... It was only when we moved to Y [northern city] that we really got any kind of – knowing a lot – of lesbians, and lesbians in different areas, ... You've got your discussion group and then you've got little social groups from that. So you make more friends ...

Bella, b. 1947, was given the number for Lesbian Line:
First of all I went to ... meet, they were supposed to be having this session for coming-out lesbians, something like that, and I went down, ... I was the only woman that turned up. These two women were there and they felt totally embarrassed and they said they had a tape, would I like to see it, and I said yes. Then they tried to put the tape on and the tape

wouldn't work, so I left! I was so heartbroken because I was still none the wiser, I was still coming away with nothing, you know!

Then I rang Lesbian Line and met them in the bar and I went down, and then I started going to the bar.

The scene: clubs and pubs

The part played by lesbian clubs such as The Gateways in London and women-only spaces during the 1960s, 70s and 80s is reported here. Also given are recollections of the contacts and support from lesbian organisations like Lesbian Lines which had been the direct result of gay rights campaigning.

Chloe, *b.1933, said of the early 1960s:*
... I'd no idea there was any *scene*, because there wasn't, in a way – there was no overt scene, as far as I was concerned, although of course you hear about the – whatever club it was in London [the Gateways], and that was going from the – before the 1900s, wasn't it?

Doreen, *b. 1931, went to the Gateways in the late 1950s/early 60s:*
Through friends that she [her partner] knew ... we got into the Gateways and met up with quite a few different people then, and we made friends ...

Well, it was, at first it was an eye-opener because I had no idea about this side of life at all, and I was still learning things, even at my age, I was ... thirties then.

But it was wonderful because you could do ... I mean, you weren't muckin' about or anything but you could dance and things like that, – you were relaxed, you were yourself, you weren't having to watch what you said, not that I ever did watch what I said! – but... you didn't have to sort of think, 'Will they think "What am I?"' You knew everybody there – well, on the whole – everybody there were in the same boat. You didn't have to pretend. You could just be natural, natter, have a few beers and things like that, ... because you could sit and talk, it wasn't too noisy and you knew that people were there were genuine ...

Chris, *b. 1947:*
I went down the Gateways Club [in 1971] with heels, nylons, well, it would have been tights, ... and this Harris tweed suit and make-up, and I went to the bar and this big butch lesbian came over and chatted me up. And I shat myself! I let her buy me a drink, and we chatted. And she said how wonderful it was to see, um – a femme. ... but I never wore a skirt again. Not down the Gateways.

Alison, b. 1946:
So then I started to hang around with any lesbians in London that I knew, because there were quite a few, I slowly realised, actually at this Women's Centre, but I never quite knew what to do – or how to behave, …

The other thing I remember doing in London is going to Gateways Club – just went the once, and I went with these two friends, … and it was extremely exciting, but I was terrified as well- 'cos – Gateways was well known for the big ogre on the door! And so you got in and it was very very dark you could hardly see what was going on ! And there were – sort of butch women and femme women and … it was – partly, – it was quite predatory and scary, but then I knew nothing about what was going on, but it was a very exciting evening.

Judith, b. 1934, described her experiences in a northern city from the early 1960s, including going to her first lesbian party:
So I was well tanked up … and I walked in and it was wonderful, I just felt immediately at home.

I wasn't in the scene at all, … I knew two women who lived in X [town] and I knew – staff where I was working [were lesbian]. Apart from that, I suppose like so many people I was doing my hunting or being hunted outside my home area, because I think a lot of professional women do that!

[There was] lots going on, joined various clubs, paid my fee there, if the police came and closed you down then you went and joined another club, as happened many times.

Certainly the first two I went to really were mixed. … one was a bit more slummy but was more fun actually, – the girl I went with, I used to sit cheek by jowl with some drag queens, they were great fun and very kind actually, … We met in – can't remember the name of the club, it was obviously underground and mainly men and they allowed you in once a month on a Friday. [Another club] … it was too rough a do. [A partner] – used to go there regularly and she's pointed out the bit of the canal she threw someone into! It was rough, …

We used to meet, … above a terrible, filthy pub upstairs, and you had to pass by all these men sitting with their beer mugs staring at the staircase as you went up. It had about fifty members, … it was principally social, you know, chatting, just meeting and chatting. But there were one or two occasions when the respectability slipped!

After being involved with lesbian groups Judith lost touch until the later 1980s:
I suddenly decided that I'd get back into the swing of things again. ... I just wanted the lesbian contact, not for anything in particular but ... you like being on the same wavelength as other people.

So I phoned up Gay Switchboard in Manchester and they me put onto Lesbian Line or the equivalent, and they put me onto Y... So I went to the second meeting [of *NOLN*], and went on from there. At the same time I had my ears pierced, – rite of passage and all the rest of it, and so I got into the swing of things again!

Colette:
I went to my first gay pub at 19, and that was around 1979. ... and I can tell you the hardcore butches terrified the shit out of me. ... I was absolutely terrified of these women, which pushed me into outwardly looking quite butch and very quickly I had my own protection.

Margot, b. 1947:
We used to go to this club ... in Stockport – called The Gaslight. ... It was a mixed club – but it was frequented by quite a lot of lesbians. ... We used to go to a club in Leeds. We used to go to clubs, lesbian clubs. ... And now ... I go circle dancing, and lesbians and hets go, not many men, ... But there is some women-only circle dancing, which tends to attract more lesbians, – in some ways I like that, but I like the other as well.

Laura, b. 1961, comments on the scene in the mid-1980s in the north-east:
I wasn't exactly looking on the scene, if that's what you could describe it as. But the scene in – we're talking X [provincial town] – is absolutely – It's based around women-only discos but they're – there's an awful lot of young – bottle-wielding – lesbians that are jumping in and out of bed with each other on a very casual basis, and we very quickly decided this was not what we wanted.

Lesley, b. 1958, outlines some typical activities of contact groups and informal networking in the early 1990s:
When I first moved up here the Y [a pub]was running … Because what it provided was a venue … it had informally grown up over time although I'm sure Lesbian Line had put energy into promoting it.

You could turn up and there would be your best friends there, who you might not have seen all week. So you could catch up with them, but also women in a much more wider extended network who you wouldn't maybe see if you didn't go to the pub. So you might end up standing at the bar and talking to somebody who you knew 'cause you'd met them at something else or they were a friend of somebody else, and catching up with them. But also women you hadn't known at all who you met again just by the networking that went on there.

… At that point it was classed as a Lesbian Line night. … Lesbian Line met women there (who['d] rang up the Line) … occasionally I saw people I know who worked on the Line with women, and they introduced me to these new women. … It wasn't a closed night, so anybody could come into the pub, … There were on average I suppose about 40 lesbians in there, you could have more in on a good night. … It was one of those things where you could drop in for ten minutes and have a quick drink, or you could stay, – the whole evening, – and it was also excellent for promoting things.

… And through the pub, I met Z and for some reason at that point there was no lesbian newsletter in X and we thought it might be a good idea, given we knew a few things were going on, to have a newsletter and so we set [one] up… And whether it was partly the Y [pub] or whether it was partly having the newsletter, a lot of different things started taking off in X, – walking group took off, – a wine-tasting group – a reading group at one point as well and – lots of different events as well that were more one-off, so I was part of a small group of women who organised a Lesbian Health day, for example. *NOLN* started around that time.

… Partly often I organise things that *I* want to go to. … I enjoy being part of them, so I go to lots of things as a participant. But through that I've met an ever-widening bigger group of lesbians, and I really value that, – I don't want to be a lesbian who just has a relationship or a lesbian who has a small group of friends, I really enjoy, I value, being a lesbian who has a much wider group of lesbians who I know as friends.

Lesbian networks: belonging and identity

Women report their feelings of trepidation before making contact and relief and pleasure at being accepted. Others expressed the view that at times they'd felt some pressure to conform to particular images of lesbians. Aspects of identity such as class and education were mentioned as part of a complex picture and a warning that simply because women are lesbians it doesn't mean that they have much in common.

Olive, *b 1934, had not belonged to any kind of lesbian community until the early 1990s:*
We got involved with – one of the [religious] women's groups, and we did meet somebody who – had said, …'Oh, is X your partner?' you see. 'Yes'. So she sort of said, well, 'Snap'. So that really was a start, because I think probably through her we've got to know more lesbian individuals and lesbian couples. So there has been a sort of – not exactly a circuit, but a group of us who now know each other – just really within the area, – and we do things together.

… Well, there *is* some affinity, I think, but – this is curious really because – the question always arises in my mind, – 'Would I have liked you if you were straight?' And the answer doesn't always have to be 'Yes!' … Or 'No!'

So since that time we've had a much wider circle of lesbian friends than we had before, and we're very happy with that.

Mary, *b. 1947 describes visiting a lesbian community in the 1980s:*
I went to the States to visit a friend of mine, and there they all were, living together, do's and things and it was suddenly like … wow!

Mary amplified her feelings, saying in her 30s she'd taken about four years to become at ease with her own identity:
Then, when I went to the first disco at, in Y [northern city], I thought well maybe I'm *not* [a lesbian] because they just seemed up on another planet. Because they were all… very butch… leathers, shaved hair, – very, very short hair, and quite aggressive, that's how it felt. And so it took me some time – to gain my own identity rather than an identity – because I didn't fit into the identity that, that I was also seeing … outside.

... The other thing was that all the people that I did know, lesbians – were vegetarian, and so again I thought, well I don't *fit in* here, you know, so it took me several years before I ... realised I could be *me*, and not have to be a vegetarian and a non-smoking non-drinking [lesbian] – it was only the people that I then had met. ... So – I was floundering as to my identity. I mean not lesbian as far as sexuality was concerned but as far as whether I fitted into – the group that were the people that [I] met.

As time went on I had this – the strength of character or whatever to accept that – *I am as I am* and this is my sexuality and I don't have to conform to all these patterns.

Because the other thing was that there was a period of time where opting out and going on benefits etcetera – seemed to be the thing that everybody was doing and I had a job and a house and ran a big – well, big car compared with everybody else, ... And I never had any problem, it wasn't like I was disapproving of them doing that, that was fine. ... but I met, oh there were lots of people and some of them – were quite rude, really, to me, – because I was so – conformist, I suppose they saw me as.

... But again, I would have been dishonest to myself if I'd tried to fit in – with them. I got *on* all right with them and some of them accepted me, some of them were rude! but that was all right.

I mean the other thing of course is the class thing. – I *was* brought up middle class, I *am* middle class and – I haven't got a problem with that. I haven't got a problem with working class either because I actually went to school in the East End of London where the majority of the pupils and my friends *were* working class, ... and you know, I still say, yes, I might have been privileged but I didn't have a choice.

***Caitlin**, b. 1957, recalled an initial awareness of one type of lesbian life and reflected on changes from the 1980s to 90s:*
I remember ... hitching up to Hebden Bridge ... and there were two women living together and they had a sort of smallholding ... and feeling very comfortable. ...It was accepted that they went to bed together. They gave me the next room, and they went to bed together, and I thought, 'Yes, right. That's it.' It's what I accepted.

During the 90s you felt that coldness, ... And then I realised cliques were forming, cliques had come out of the woodwork from the crushing days of Thatcherism. Age – age was an important factor. … Lifestyle [politics] came along. … less debating, less theorising, which I think is very important for us. You know – 'Why are we going down this line? Why are we using these categories which are defining each other? … And by the 90s I felt the open, flexible women's communities had gone.

Georgina, b. 1951:
There was lots of things in London, and one of the things that I really got into and fascinated about was the difference between white lesbianism, and black lesbianism and because – and because of my work that was made easier for me because I worked with black women and white women. Some of the white women were lesbians, some of the black women were lesbians, and that was really really interesting, in terms of culture and music as well as politics, and the books that were around then.

And I was at an age – I was in my thirties, – lots of energy, it was very exciting, lots was happening around, – the lesbian scene, it was a really good time. Probably any year is a good time when you come out as a lesbian, but it was a good time for me.

Yeah, I think one of the things about my lesbian identity that I know... is, I continue to need, – is knowing other lesbians. I need to and want to live all my life aspects – with other lesbians there and – I don't know if that's true for everybody.

In that connection *NOLN*, [has] been a great help to me and to my lesbian identity. Because the women that I've met through that, not necessarily have become friends, but the things that have been shared from different women in workshops I've found very powerful. On the one hand it's sort of broadened my understanding of – different ways different women come to lesbianism but also it's – strengthens my identity as being part of a very rich and varied community.

And that's quite reinforcing for me – and helps me know, -'cause of this thing that, 'Oh well, all lesbians are the same, if you only know lesbians you're leading a very narrow life, aren't you'. And, it helps me know there's another truth …

Frances, b. 1953. On her lesbian identity:
I think my feminism does [have an impact], I think that's more what really impacts on everything, – Well my political philosophy, really, I mean

that actually makes more of a difference but then that's part of who I am as a lesbian, so – you can't separate them – I can't separate them.

But really it's not just about what I do in bed and with who, you know it's something more about identity – female identity, female friendships, female relationships.

… I mean I really admire the women that went before 'cos I think they must have had it a lot harder – and I think you know we've got a lot to thank them for really 'cos I think they did actually make a – make a lesbian culture.

Bella, b. 1947 had contacted Lesbian Line and met a contact in a pub:
I mean this is totally new to me, going into a pub … and getting a drink and actually joining somebody … it was just seeing somebody that you could talk to, and I did actually feel that women were sort of in cliques and it was very difficult to get into a group or whatever.

One night X said to me, 'I wonder what it's like coming in', and I said it was dreadful, it was absolutely terrible. And from then on she [X] had a stool at a table, … After that, I could move about and mingle, but I just had to have that, that thing, that place. … I could actually sort of feel the energy and feel fantastic.

I joined everything, I joined everything. I went to *NOLN*, I was at the Dykes' Diner, the walking group, wine tasting, I was in everything, I just joined everything. I got to know lots of women. Yes. And within a year, really, I was a year on my own in a flat – and I was doing lots of things.

Bella describes sharing a house with other lesbians:
That was much better, there was loads of women coming and going, and I got more into sort of living with dykes and that was great, actually, fantastic.

Lesley, spoke about debates on class in the 1980s:
[I'll] Give you an example from a workshop at a conference I went to, … I think it was around lesbian sex and sexuality … and as part of that there was a debate going on. … A young woman said that she particularly targeted and got involved with slightly older women who she knew were, – not very out, … And she basically felt it was fine to get them to pay for everything, … Because – her solidarity was a class solidarity, not necessar-

ily a lesbian solidarity. And I can remember being incredibly shocked by that – for me I suppose lesbian solidarity was the bigger issue, and I don't know whether actually she did it to provoke debate.

But there were lots of issues about, and lots of language that was being developed then, so there was one idea about vanilla sex which was supposed to be a very tame way in which many lesbians related to each other sexually, and that we should be moving beyond that into a whole range of different sexual experiences. I remember … we went to this conference and both of us, our minds were getting blown! by all of this stuff, really,

Terri, b. 1941, when 37:
I came out into a kind of very separatist feminist environment, and in no time at all, – there were lesbian separatist conferences and all that sort of thing. I didn't actually go to any of those [consciousness-raising groups] 'cause I lived in a very isolated place, but I was very around that sort of stuff.

I eventually started going to Y [northern city], and I went to the lesbian discos there. That was my social scene, yeah. And I – the music was very, very important.

… Where I'd come from was the Y [northern city] scene, which was a very destructive scene, really – I mean there was a lot of – smashed windows – a lot of … class warfare, really bad class warfare, … Because I was working class, I found it very difficult to find my place, … I was angry about class and I did come out with some really heavy duty stuff, but I didn't have that kind of hatred … and so I never knew where to be …

And we [Terri and partner] went into this bar and… started having a drink and a woman who sat next to me said, 'Are you a feminist?' And I, thinking that that was a good thing to be, said, 'Yes.' You know – sitting up straight and being all proud – and she said, 'Oh, I thought as much. We don't want your sort in here, you're spoiling it for us.'

In the 1980s:
I – managed to get a farmhouse to rent and – lived in isolation … Quite a lot of women used to come and go … women used to come out from the cities, from different cities – and used to stay with me for the weekend. We used to talk politics, sometimes, or we would talk about sex, or sexuality, for a whole weekend, – go for walks on the fells and talk, talk, talk.

So I felt – I think I felt more confident in myself ... I started to understand that being older was like being sometimes actually admired rather
than it being a negative thing. That women were actually looking for role
models. And the fact that I was independent and lived on my own in the
middle of beautiful countryside was a sort of bit of a role model, in some
ways. So that also gave me a positive sense of myself.

Alison, b. 1946, reflected on the lesbian world:
So I suppose relationships-wise I – it took me a long time really to adapt,
I think, to the lesbian world. – I went through a lot of heartache, because
everything was different, there weren't any roles and – it was very easy to
fall in love and – think that was it forever! – and then either get cheated
on or for it all to wear off, – I just went through a lot of heartache in the
lesbian world and a lot of growing up, really, 'cause I'd had very idealistic
ideas about – relationships between women were going to be absolutely
wonderful, because of course women wouldn't exploit each other like men
exploited women.

And unfortunately I had my eyes opened to that, that women are human
beings too! And we exploit each other. So I had a lot – of learning and
growing up to do about the lesbian world. And a lot of thinking too,
because in the 70s there was a lot of talk about non-monogamy and
monogamy was wrong, in inverted commas, and jealousy was wrong and
we were all trained to be friends, lovers, companions to everybody, and, –
basically it was too hard. It didn't seem to work for me, anyway.

Some people maybe can do it, but I found it really hard, and basically I
wanted, I suppose, really, something still along the heterosexual ... *model,* –
I had to admit in the end that I wanted to be monogamous and in the end
I wanted somebody to live with, but it took a long time to work all that
out and to think what I really wanted as opposed to what I thought was
the ideal and what I *should* be doing.

Louisa, b. 1951:
Being lesbian is one of the main reasons for moving to [north]. I'd got to
a point in my life where I wanted to live where there was a good community of women. It didn't necessarily have to be lesbian women, but a good
strong community of women. And I knew there were hundreds of dykes
up this end!

I've always really liked this area, so that's one of the main reasons for moving over here, and I didn't know anybody when I moved. Then I went on [a] Homophobia Awareness training course, ... because I thought I might meet people, and I did.

And X told me about *NOLN*, and since I went to *NOLN* I've thought, 'This is why I came to Y!' .... and I like living somewhere that there are a lot of lesbians. So I think moving ... and finding *NOLN* has been a very important time in my life, and it is a very – well, it's still ongoing, you know. The honeymoon hasn't ended yet! ...

And finally, some reflections on the expectation that all lesbians will have a lot in common.

Margot, b. 1947:
I have friends of all kinds, and I don't really believe that lesbians necessarily have the answer to things that I need. I find some of them have ... I find some of them I don't get on with, and I don't have to pretend to get on with them just because they're lesbians. ... And I have a lot of close friends that *are* lesbians, a lot of close friends that aren't, and a couple of close friends that are men ...

I think that was a turning point, when I was 40, I thought ... I haven't that much time left and I'm going to spend it with people I want to spend it with, regardless of who they are, and I'm going to read what I want, regardless of whether it's right on or not. ... So – I'm different now. Much happier. Much more – clear.

Mary, b. 1947:
Because the other thing is, that the fact that we *do* – lesbians come in all shapes and sizes, and all different sorts of people and ... you wouldn't do it if you were *het*erosexual, thinking that you would get on with everybody and fit in. ... And although there's a *plus* I think in being lesbian in the fact that you are exposed to a much wider – range of people than you ever would be if you were heterosexual, you can be exposed to them but not actually have to fit in.

Conclusions

- Most of the women we interviewed had experienced homophobia in one form or another.

- Although they were aware of discrimination and bigotry, some acquiesced in conventional mores by keeping their sexual orientation secret for many years. This was particularly so for older women, born in the 1930s and 40s.

- Homophobia had both direct and tangential effects. It was detrimental to some women's sense of identity. Others reacted by challenging homophobia and at some point it helped galvanise them into political action.

- Besides personal preference, external influences such as geographical location, stage of life and the wax and wane of equal rights campaigns impacted on possibilities for involvement in any visible gay culture and/or political activism.

- Several participants made links between lesbianism and feminism.

- The majority of the interviewees translated their feelings about their gender and sexual orientation into action to promote equality and justice. Their work and achievements for women's and gay rights have benefited many individuals and communities.

- In the early stages of the development of their lesbian identity some women felt very isolated. Several found initial contact with lesbians *en masse* an alienating experience.

- Lesbian 'contact' organisations such as Lesbian Lines proved invaluable for some.

- The gay 'scene' provided a lively social life for many.

- Networks – of friends, work colleagues, members of gay and women's organisations – were very significant. Many participants articulated their sense of relief at finding like-minded women.

- While many women expressed appreciation of lesbian company, it was acknowledged that not all gay women and men necessarily had much in common other than identifying as lesbians or gay.

Glossary

Some brief explanations of words and terms used by interviewees.

Identity(ies): the individual characteristics by which a person can be identified; the many elements in an individual's personality or roles which an individual inhabits; a person's sense of who she/he is.

Politicization: a process of becoming aware of and informed about politics and how politics affect many aspects of social life.

Coming out: "to declare openly one's homosexuality" (*Chambers Dictionary*) – see the section on coming out in our booklet, Lesbians on … Becoming Our Selves.

Political lesbians: those who believe that sexual practice should follow their political principles regarding gender relationships, sometimes used in a derogatory sense.

The scene: a general term used to describe gay culture and social activities.

Het: jargon for hetereosexual attitudes and behaviour, particularly those which are assumed to be the norm.

Homophobia: a strong aversion to or hatred of homosexual people, particularly when acted upon. Lesbophobic views focus on lesbians and lesbian activity.

Internalised homophobia: When the prevailing culture of fear and condemnation of gays and lesbians is absorbed (often unconsciously) by an individual.

Clause and Section 28: part of legislation introduced in Local Government Acts of 1988 which proposed and then brought into law several elements discriminating against homosexuals, for example, banning the "promotion" of homosexuality in schools.

Feminism: beliefs advocating women's rights and opportunities, particularly those which challenge inequalities between the sexes in society.

Second-wave women's movement: often known as the Women's Liberation Movement, a follow-on from the 19th century campaigns for women's emancipation, which re-emerged in the late 1960s. Some of the main issues were equal pay for equal work, sexual and reproductive rights, freedom from sexual violence and abuse.

Radical feminism: feminist ideas which recommend a revolutionary overthrow of unjust social structures rather than reform.

Separatists: feminists and lesbians who advocate that women should live completely separate lives from men.

Consciousness raising: a key feature of the second-wave women's liberation movement whereby women met to analyse gender relationships, explore their feelings and support each other. The slogan: "the personal is political" represents many of the beliefs springing from this process.

Greenham: a peace camp run and sustained by women, protesting against Cruise Missiles at a US air base at Greenham Common, Berkshire, during the 1980s onwards.

Lesbian Lines: lesbian contact organisations which provide various services for lesbians, from running a telephone help and contact line to organising social events and raising finance to support lesbian action.

NOLN: Northern Older Lesbian Network; now the Northern Lesbian Network.

Appendix I
The interviews

All the women interviewed for the Project were volunteers, as are the Women's Oral History Group members. The interviews ranged in length from half-an-hour to over an hour and the audiotapes were then transcribed.

This is an oral history record, not a quantitative survey. However, here are a few statistics to give you an idea of the participants.

The women we interviewed
Age at interview

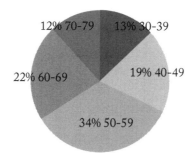

Class and ethnicity

Those interviewed were not asked about class or nationality/ethnic background. Many volunteered this information themselves, so this was categorised as: self-defined or very strongly implied. Although we searched for lesbians with a greater variety of ethnic origin and for younger women, we did not receive many volunteers from these categories unfortunately.

Working class: 15. Middle class 11. Not mentioned: 6

Mostly British, 4 born outside UK; mostly, but not all, white.

Place of birth/where they spent childhood

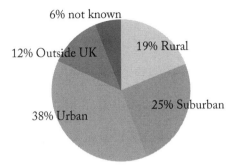

Nearly 94% of the participants moved away from the area where they grew up; just over 6% stayed within their home area.

The majority (94%) had lived in London or other large cities, including over 37% who lived abroad at some point.

Education

87.5% of participants went to university, college or trained for a professional qualification, several as mature students; 12.5% completed secondary education only.

Heterosexual relationships

About 37% had been married or had had long-term heterosexual relationships; 28% are mothers, some are grandmothers.

Involvement in organisations

Most of the participants were and/or are involved with various organisations or activism.

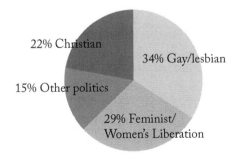

Appendix II
Our oral history project: The group's process

How it all began:

What prompted the Women's Oral History Lesbian Identity Project was a realisation that is very difficult to find the stories of lesbian women in the past. This became more apparent to us after a few lesbians tried to put together a display about lesbians in history for the Bradford Mela (multicultural festival). So we, as LIP, set about creating a record of and for lesbians at the end of the 20th century.

About the participants:

We advertised throughout the north of England for women who identified as lesbian and would be willing to be recorded talking about their lives and the formulation of their lesbian identity.

How we organised and conducted the interviews:

The next phase was a long and protracted one. It comprised lengthy discussions about how we might conduct the interviews. We also discussed and took guidance on how to be non-directive in our interviewing approach and adjusted our interviewing technique in the light of a number of pilot interviews. In the end we opted for a loose structure and a list of questions to be used as prompts which we used very flexibly. After the interviews, women were asked to read through a transcript to confirm accuracy.

Analysis:

The next stage was to work out how to present the massive amount of material that had been collected. We decided to keep full oral records of all interviews and produce a series of booklets containing a selection of quotations. This involved researching various methods of analysis. By listening to the interview tapes and reading the transcripts again and again we saw themes emerge. The major themes began to crystallise. Some of them were what would have been expected given the nature of the Project, others emerged spontaneously, such as the role of religion in the participants' lives. Then we collected together the women's actual words in relation to chosen themes and allocated a number of themes to each booklet. In this part of the process we made great efforts to present without any bias what women said and to produce booklets which were readable, although we are aware that, of itself, an editing process requires selecting, organising and reordering.

Goals achieved:

Along the way we met various methodological, organisation and technical challenges! For those who would like to know more about this process, further information is available from the Group. Over the course of the project, we have spoken to several groups, produced a display for the first national conference for older lesbians and given a presentation at a Public History Conference at Ruskin College, Oxford. The first of our four booklets was distributed in June 2009, the next two were launched in February 2010 and this, the final booklet was produced towards the end of that year. The audio tapes have been digitised and transferred to CDs and will be lodged in archives.

The tapes represent nearly 30 hours of oral record and contain much more than we have been able to include in our booklets. There are endless possibilities to look afresh at the stories we have collected and to find new themes, insights and gems.

The other LIP booklets are:

Lesbians ... and Christianity ISB No. 978-0-9561331-0-6

Lesbians on ... Choosing Our Icons ISB No. 978-0-9561331-1-3

Lesbians on ... Becoming Our Selves ISB No. 978-0-9561331-2-0

Notes

1. Attempting to simplify a complex subject, we've used the word 'lesbian' to mean women who love women and have same-sex erotic relationships.

2. We have tried to preserve anonymity for our interviewees. Names have been changed when requested although some were happy to have their names included. Identifiable details such as names of partners or location have been represented by X, Y or Z.

3. Some extracts could have appeared under a number of sections. To maintain narrative coherence and bring out the individual 'voice' they've been presented more fully in one place.

4. We have used the words actually spoken by participants. Occasionally, for clarity we indicate (in different type or in square brackets) context, chronology or topic.

5. The usual custom of a gap with three full-stops indicates that some words have been omitted. This has been done to clarify narrative, e.g. when a speaker goes off on a tangent, then returns to the original topic. Repetitions – 'you know', 'sort of' and disfluencies such as 'er', 'um' etc. have usually been removed to help narrative flow; hesitations marked with a small dash.

We welcome feedback ...

The LIP group welcomes feedback on any issue raised in the booklets. Please address any comments to the address below.

The archive of the original audiotapes and transcripts will be accessible to accredited researchers.

For further information, please contact:

LIP Women's Oral History Group
C/o. The Equity Centre
Perkins House
1 Longlands Street
BRADFORD BD1 2TP